Anthony Shaffer

SLEUTH
A Play

Marion Boyars
London · New York

Published in Great Britain and the United States in 1977 by
MARION BOYARS PUBLISHERS
26 Parke Road London SW13 9NG

First published in 1971 by Calder & Boyars Ltd
Reprinted by Marion Boyars 1981, 1985, 1988, 1992, 1998, 2004, 2009,
2013, 2013, 2019, 2022

www.marionboyars.co.uk

Printed in 2022
10 9 8 7 6 5 4 3
© Anthony Shaffer 1971

A CIP catalogue record for this book is available from the British Library.
A CIP catalog record for this book is available from the Library of Congress.

ISBN 10 digit 0-7145-0763-6 Paperback
ISBN 13 digit 978-0-7145-0763-7 Paperback

Printed and bound in England by the Short Run Press, Exeter

To: Father Brown, Mr. Philip Trent, Mr. Max Carrados, Dr. Reginald Fortune, Mr. Roger Sheringham, Mr. Albert Campion, Mr. Nigel Strangeways, Lord Peter Wimsey, Dr. Gideon Fell, Monsieur Hercule Poirot, and all their omniscient, eccentric, amateur gentlemen colleagues, this play is dedicated with sincere regard and affection.

Illustrations from the

Palomar Pictures Production of

SLEUTH

Presented by 20th Century-Fox

starring

Laurence Olivier and Michael Caine

screenplay

Anthony Shaffer based upon his play

Produced by Morton Gottlieb

Directed by Joseph L. Mankiewicz

Released in the United Kingdom by
Fox-Rank Distributors Ltd.

SLEUTH

SLEUTH was first presented at the St. Martin's Theatre, London, on February 12th, 1970, after a pre-London tour of Oxford, Leeds, Brighton and Eastbourne, with the following cast:

ANDREW WYKE	Anthony Quayle
MILO TINDLE	Keith Baxter
INSPECTOR DOPPLER	Stanley Rushton
DET. SGT. TARRANT	Robin Mayfield
P. C. HIGGS	Liam McNulty

The play was directed by Clifford Williams.

ACT ONE

(The curtain rises on the living room of ANDREW WYKE's Norman Manor House in Wiltshire. It is stone flagged, and a tall window runs the height of the back wall. It is divided laterally by a minstrels gallery which, in turn, is approached by a winding staircase. A wardrobe, stage left, and a grandfather clock, and bureau stage right stand on the gallery. Upstage right is the hallway leading to the unseen front door. Upstage left a corridor leads into another part of the house. Standing in this corridor is a basket. Games of all kinds adorn the room ranging in complexity from chess, draughts and chequers, to early dice and card games and even earlier blocking games like Senat and Nine Men Morris. Upstage centre, by the window, under the gallery is a full-sized "Laughing Sailor".

As the play opens ANDREW WYKE, is sitting at his desk, typing. He is a strongly built, tall, fleshy man of 57, gone slightly to seed. His fair hair carries on it the suspicion that chemical aid has been invoked to keep the grey at bay. His face, sourly amused and shadowed with evaded self-knowledge is beginning to reflect the absence of constant, arduous employment. He wears a smoking jacket and black tie.

The clock strikes eight o'clock. ANDREW turns to look at clock, finishes typing, takes the page from the typewriter and begins to read)

ANDREW. "Since you appear to know so much, Lord Merridew, Sir," said the Inspector humbly, "I wonder if you could explain just how the murderer managed to leave the body of his victim in the middle of the Tennis Court, and effect his escape without leaving any tracks behind him in the red dust. Frankly, sir, we in the Police Force are just plain baffled. There seems no way he could have done it, short of black magic. " St. John Lord Merridew, the great detective, rose majestically, his huge Father Christmas face, glowing with mischievous delight. Slowly he brushed the crumbs of seedy cake from the folds of his pendulous waistcoat. "The police may be baffled, Inspector, " he boomed, "but Merridew is not. It's all a question of a little research and a little ratiocination. Thirty years ago, the murderer, Doctor Grayson, was a distinguished member of the Ballet Russe dancing under the name of Oleg Graysinski. The years may have altered his appearance, but his old skill had not deserted him. He carried the body out to the centre of the tennis court, walking on his points along the white tape which divides the services boxes. From there he threw it five feet into the court, towards the base line, where it was found, and then, with a neatly executed fouette, faced about and returned the way he had come, thus leaving no traces. There, Inspector, that is Merridew's solution. "

Splendid! Absolutely splendid! Merridew loses none of his cunning I'm glad to say. He's as neat <u>and</u> as gaudy as ever he was.

(The doorbell rings. ANDREW finishes his drink slowly, then exits to hallway)

Oh hallo. Good evening, Milo Tindle, is it?

MILO. Yes. Mr. Wyke?

ANDREW. Yes. Do come in won't you?

MILO. Thank you.

(The front door is heard to close. ANDREW walks back into the room. He is followed by MILO TINDLE.

He is about 35, slim, dark-haired and of medium
height. He has a sharp, sallow face alive with a faintly
Mediterranean wariness. Everything about him is neat
from his exactly parted hair to the squared off white
handkerchief in the breast pocket of his blue mohair
suit)

ANDREW. Let me take your coat.

(ANDREW hangs coat on coat rack U. L.)

Did you find the entrance to the lane alright?

MILO. Yes.

(MILO walks about surveying room)

ANDREW. Well done. Most people go straight past it. It's
very nice of you to come.

MILO. Not at all. I found your note when I got down from
London this afternoon.

ANDREW. Oh good. I pushed it through your letter box.

MILO. Er ... What's this? (Indicating life-size figure of a
sailor sitting in front of window)

ANDREW. Oh that's Jolly Jack Tar the Jovial Sailor. He
and I have a very good relationship. I make the jokes
and he laughs at them. (He moves the sailor's head
manually) You see ha ha! Now let me get you a drink.
(Moves to drinks trolley) What will you have? Scotch,
Gin, Vodka?

MILO. Scotch.

ANDREW. How do you like it? Soda, water, ice?

MILO. Just ice. And what's this?

(MILO has crossed to table D. L. C. on which there
is a large game)

ANDREW. Oh that's a game.

MILO. It looks like a child's game. (He picks up one
of the pieces)

ANDREW. It's anything but childish I can assure you. I've
been studying it for months, and I'm still only a
novice. It's called Senat, played by the Ancient Egyp-
tians. It's an early blocking game, not unlike our own
Nine Men Morris. Would you mind putting that back
where you found it. It's taken me a long time to get
it there. How are you settling in at Laundry Cottage?

MILO. Very well.

ANDREW. Using it for weekends, that sort of thing?

MILO. Yes, that's the sort of thing.

ANDREW. It's a charming little place. Well, cheers.

MILO. Cheers.

ANDREW. Now do come and sit down. Forgive me if I
just tidy up a bit. I've just reached the denouement of
my new book. "The Body On the Tennis Court". Tell
me would you agree that the detective story is the
normal recreation of noble minds?

MILO. Who said that?

ANDREW. Oh I'm quoting Philip Guedalla. A biographer
of the thirties. The golden age when every cabinet
minister had a thriller by his bedside, and all the
detectives were titled. Before your time I expect.

MILO. Perhaps it would have been truer to say that noble
minds were the normal recreation of detective story
writers.

ANDREW. Yes. Good point. You know even in these days I
still set my own work among the gentry. And a great
number of people enjoy it, in spite of the Welfare
State.

14

MILO. I'm surprised they haven't done any of your stuff on television.

ANDREW. Oh God forbid.

MILO. Well they're always doing crime stories.

ANDREW. What - you mean those ghastly things where the police race around in cars and call all the suspects chummy?

MILO. Yes. That's the kind of thing.

ANDREW. Oh no that's not my line of country at all. That is detective fact not detective fiction.

MILO. And of course as such is of much less interest to noble minds.

ANDREW. Yes, yes you've put it in a nut shell, my dear Milo, if I may so address you.

MILO. Of course.

ANDREW. Thank you, we need to be friendly. Now do sit down and let me get you another drink. I'm one up on you already.

(MILO starts to sit in chair below staircase.

ANDREW moves to drinks table)

I understand you want to marry my wife.

(A pause. MILO is disconcerted by the directness of the question)

You'll forgive me raising the matter, but as Marguerite is away for a few days, she's up in the North you know visiting some relatives...

MILO. Is she?

ANDREW. Yes, so I thought it an appropriate time for a

little chat.

MILO. Yes.

ANDREW. Well is it true?

MILO. Well ... Well, yes, with your permission of course.

ANDREW. Oh yes of course. (He crosses to MILO) Zere, put zat behind your necktie.

MILO. Cheers.

ANDREW. Prosit. (He stands in front of the fireplace) Yes I'm glad to see you're not like so many young men these days seem to think they can do anything they like without asking anyone's permission.

MILO. Certainly not.

ANDREW. Good. I'm pleased to hear it. I know you won't object then if I ask you a few questions about your parents and so on.

MILO. My mother was born in Hereford, a farmer's daughter. My father is an Italian who came to this country in the thirties.

ANDREW. Jewish?

MILO. Half, on his mother's side, that for the Fascists was the important side. The male they felt didn't transmit the disease so virulently.

ANDREW. (tut-tutting) Dreadful business, dreadful.

MILO. Of course I'm not at all religious myself, I'm an agnostic.

ANDREW. (crosses to centre stage) My dear boy, you don't have to explain to me. We're all liberals here. I have no prejudice against Jews, or even half-Jews. Why some of my best friends are half-Jews ... Mind

16

you I hope you have no objections to any children that
you and my wife may have being brought up Church
of England?

MILO.   None whatsoever if that's what Marguerite wants.

ANDREW.   You haven't discussed it yet?

MILO.   Not yet, it doesn't seem to have cropped up.

ANDREW.   Well I suppose in some ways that's rather a
relief. But if you take my advice you'll opt for C of
E. It's so much simpler. A couple of hours on Christmas Eve and Good Friday and you've seen the whole
thing off nicely. And if you throw in Remembrance
Sunday they give you the good Christian medal with
oak leaf cluster.

MILO.   It's the same with a lot of Jews. My father used to
say 'most people only talk to their really old friends
two or three times a year. Why should God be angry
if He gets the same treatment?'

ANDREW.   (insincerely) Very amusing. Your father? Was
his name Tindle? It doesn't sound very Italian.

MILO.   He name was Tindolini. But if you had a name like
that in England in those days you had to make a-da-nice
cream. He was a watch-maker and so he changed it.

ANDREW.   Was he a successful man?

MILO.   No. His business failed. He went back to Italy. I
send money from time to time and go and visit him
and get a little sun or ski-ing, depending, of course,
on the season.

ANDREW.   Ah!

MILO.   It's not that I'm disloyal to Britain, you understand.
It's just that the Cairngorms and Minehead don't
offer quite the same attractions.

ANDREW.   And you? What do you do?

17

MILO. I'm in the Travel business. I have my own agency in Dulwich.

ANDREW. Tindle's Travels, eh? I see, and where do you live?

MILO. I live above the office.

ANDREW. In Dulwich?

MILO. Yes, I rent the whole house. It's really most convenient, and ... and it's most attractive, too. It's Georgian.

ANDREW. H'm. I'm sure it's perfectly delightful but I doubt whether an 18th century architectural gem in Dulwich whispers quite the same magic to Marguerite as it does to you.

MILO. She adores old houses. She can't wait to live there.

ANDREW. I understood she was already living there - at least for a couple of nights a week. I'm not mistaken, am I?

(MILO shrugs in embarrassment)

And surely your motive in renting the cottage down here was to increase the incidence of this hebdomadal coupling?

MILO. I came to be near the woman I love. It is a great pain for us to be apart. You wouldn't understand.

ANDREW. Possibly. But I understand Marguerite well enough to know that she does not adore old houses. She's lived here quite a time, and between them the rising damp and the Death Watch Beetle have put the boot into her good and proper. She's only got to see a mullioned window and it brings her out in lumps.

MILO. (hotly) Perhaps it wasn't the house so much as the person she had to share it with.

ANDREW. Now, now. I thought you were well brought up. Surely you know it's very rude to make personal remarks.

MILO. I'm sorry. You were disparaging my lover.

ANDREW. On the contrary, I was reminiscing about my wife.

MILO. It comes to the same thing.

ANDREW. Things mostly do, you know. I'll wager that within a year, it's you who will be doing the dis - paraging, and I who will be doing the rhapsodising, having quite forgotten how intolerably tiresome, vain, spendthrift, self-indulgent and generally bloody crafty she really is.

MILO. If you don't love Marguerite, you don't have to abuse her.

ANDREW. Never speak ill of the deadly eh?

MILO. Now look here ...

ANDREW. If I choose to say that my wife converses like a child of six, cooks like a Brightlingsea landlady, and makes love like a coelacanth I shall.

MILO. That's just about enough ...

ANDREW. And I certainly don't need her lover's permission to do so either. In fact, the only thing I need to know from you is, can you afford to take her off my hands?

MILO. Afford to ...

ANDREW. Afford to support her in the style to which she wasn't accustomed before she met me, but now is.

(MILO gestures around the room)

MILO. She won't need all this when we're married. It'll be a different life - a life of love and simplicity.

19

Now go ahead - sneer at that. It's almost a national sport in this country - sneering at love.

ANDREW. I don't have to sneer at it. I simply don't believe you. For Marguerite, love is the fawning of a willing lap dog, and simplicity a square cut 10-carat diamond from Van Cleef and Arpels.

(MILO rises to his feet, and moves to drinks table to put down glass)

MILO. I don't know what I'm doing here. With a little effort I'm sure you could find a much more appreciative audience.

ANDREW. Oh now, Milo. You disappoint me. Rising to your feet like that and bridling.

MILO. (abashed) I wasn't bridling. I was protesting.

ANDREW. It looked like a good old fashioned Hedy Lamarr bridle to me.

MILO. (turning to ANDREW) Who?

ANDREW. Oh very good! Very good! Why don't you just sit down and we'll talk about something that matters desperately to both of us.

ANDREW. Marguerite?

ANDREW. Money! Have you got any?

MILO. Well I'm not a millionaire, but I've got the lease on the house and some capital equipment, and the turnover in the business this year has been growing every month. By this time next year I ...

ANDREW. This year, next year, sometime never. What you're saying in fact is that at present you're skint.

20

MILO. I'll survive.

ANDREW. I'm sure you will but survival is not the point.
Presumably when you're married to Marguerite
you'll want a fast car, a little place in the sun, and
a couple of mistresses.

MILO. Why presumably? Just because you need those
things.

ANDREW. Certainly I do. And so does every right thinking
insecure, deceitful man. The point is how to get
them. (He moves to drinks table)

MILO. I'm sure you do alright. (He crosses to fire place)

ANDREW. Me? Oh no. Just this fading mansion, the
slowest Lagonda in Wiltshire, and only one mistress,
I'm afraid.

MILO. Téa? The Finnish lady who runs the Sauna Bath
at Swindon.

ANDREW. Oh, so you know about her, do you?

MILO. Marguerite and I have no secrets from each other.

ANDREW. Not even mine, it seems. (Mock mystical) Téa
is a Karelian Goddess. Her mother was Ilma,
supreme divinity of the air; her father was Jumala,
the great Creator. Her golden hair smells of pine,
and her cobalt eyes are the secret forest pools of
Finlandia.

MILO. I hear she's a scrubbed blonde with all the sex
appeal of chilled Dettol.

ANDREW. (with dignity) There are those who believe that
cleanliness is next to sexiness. And if I were you I
wouldn't pay much attention to what Marguerite says.
You can take it from me that Téa's an engaging little
trollop, and she suits me mightily. Mind you, she
takes a bit of keeping up with, it's a good thing I'm
pretty much of an Olympic sexual athlete.

21

MILO. I suppose these days you're concentrating on the sprints rather than on the long distance stuff.

ANDREW. Not so, dear boy. (He sits) I'm in the pink of condition. I could copulate for England at any distance.

MILO. Well, they do say in Olympic circles, that the point is to take part, rather than to win, so I suppose there's hope for us all. Are you going to marry her?

ANDREW. Marry a Goddess? I wouldn't presume. I might get turned into a birch tree for my audacity. Oh no I simply want to live with her.

MILO. So what's stopping you?

ANDREW. Basically the firm of Prurient and Pry Ltd., whom you and Marguerite have seen fit to employ. Don't look so innocent. Those Woodbine stained private detectives who've been camping outside Tea's flat for the last week.

MILO. (crossing to centre stage) So you spotted them?

ANDREW. A Bantu with glaucoma couldn't have missed them. No-one can read the Evening News for four hours in a Messerschmidt bubble car, and expect to remain undetected.

MILO. Sorry about that. It was Marguerite's idea.

ANDREW. Who else's? Who paid?

MILO. I did.

ANDREW. I wonder you could afford it.

MILO. It was an insurance policy against you changing your mind about divorcing Marguerite.

ANDREW. My dear boy, let us have no misunderstanding. I've nothing against you marrying Marguerite. There's nothing I want more than to see you two tucked up together. But it's got to be a fixture. I want to be rid of her for life, not just a two week Tindle Tour, economy class. No, you listen to me. You don't know her like I do. You think you do, but you don't. The real truth of the matter is that if you fail her, by which I mean cancelling the account at Harrods, or short-changing her on winter in Jamaica, she'll be back to me in a jiffy mewing for support - and guilty wife or no, she may be entitled to get it.

MILO. Don't be so bloody pathetic. Winter in Jamaica? I'm not going to take her for winter in Jamaica. You're worrying unnecessarily. Once Marguerite is married to me she'll never think of returning to you. Never. And don't worry about my being able to look after her either.

ANDREW. I see. You mean as soon as you and she are married, Marguerite will joyously exchange Cartiers for the Co-op?

MILO. So she's used to luxury. Whose fault is that?

ANDREW. It's not a fault if you can afford it. But can you? Knowing you to be hard up has she shown any sign of mending her ways in these last idyllic three months? When did she last turn down Bollinger for the blandishments of Baby cham? Or reject Crepes Suzettes in favour of Roly Poly? No, no I'm not joking, how much has this brief liaison cost you so far? £500? £800, £1,000? And that father of yours in Italy, when did you last send him any money? You see why I'm concerned. I tell you. She'll ruin you. To coin a phrase, in two years you'll be a used gourd. And what's more, a used gourd with a sizeable overdraft.

MILO. We've often talked about money. I've told her we spend too much.

ANDREW. And she takes no notice?

MILO. (low) None.

ANDREW. A silvery laugh? A coquettish turn of the head?

MILO. Something like that.

ANDREW. Exactly. Well, it's to solve this little problem
that I have invited you here tonight. This, as they
say, is where the plot thickens.

MILO. Ah!

ANDREW. I'll get you another drink.

(He crosses to drinks table. In "Listen with Mother"
style)

Are you sitting comfortably? Then I'll begin. Once
upon a time there was an Englishman called Andrew
Wyke who, in common with most of his countrymen
was virtually castrated by taxation. To avoid total
emasculation, his accountants advised him, just
before the last devaluation, to put a considerable part
of his money, some £135,000, into jewellery. His
wife, of course, was delighted.

MILO. You made her a present of it?

ANDREW. Absolutely not. It's still mine, as well she
knows. But we felt she might as well wear it, as
bank it. After all, it's fully insured.

MILO. I see what you mean by the plot thickening. It
usually does when insurance is mentioned.

ANDREW. I'm glad you follow me so readily. I want you
to steal that jewellery.

MILO. (astounded) What?

ANDREW. Tonight, for choice. Marguerite is out of the
house. It's an admirable opportunity.

MILO. You must be joking.

24

ANDREW. You would know it if I were.

MILO. (playing for time) But ... But what about the
    servants?

ANDREW. I've sent Mr. and Mrs. Hawkins to Weston-
    super-Mare for a 48 hour paddle. They won't be
    back till Sunday night. So, the house is empty.

MILO. I see.

ANDREW. What do you say?

MILO. It sounds criminal.

ANDREW. Of course it's criminal. All good money-making
    schemes in England have got to be these days. The
    jewellery, when it's not in the bank, lives in the
    safe under the stairs. It's there now. All you have to
    do is steal them, and sell them abroad and live
    happily ever after with Marguerite. All I have to do is
    to claim the insurance money and live happily ever
    after with Tēa. (Pause) Well, in my case perhaps,
    not ever after, but at least until I get fed up with a
    cuisine based on the elk.

MILO. Is that what you asked me over to hear? A scummy
    little plot to defraud the insurance company?

ANDREW. I'm sorry you find the plot scummy. I thought
    it was nicely clear and simple.

MILO. Nicely obvious and clearly unworkable. Supposing
    I do as you say and take the jewels. If I sell them to a
    fence, always supposing I could find one, I'd get a
    fraction of their value.

ANDREW. Not with the fences I know.

MILO. (derisory) What fences would you know?

ANDREW. I know some of the finest fences in Europe.
    Prudent yet prodigal. I met them some years ago

while researching "The Deadly Affair of the Druce Diamond".

MILO. Never read it.

ANDREW. You never read it! I suppose you're going to tell me you never read "Diet of Worms", or "The Mystery of the Plantaganet Parakeet"?

MILO. Sorry.

ANDREW. Haven't you read any of my books?

MILO. I'm afraid not. What were you telling me about fences?

ANDREW. That I know a great many. In fact on your behalf I have already contacted a certain gentleman in Amsterdam. He will treat you very well; you won't get full value of the jewels but you will get two-thirds, say £90,000, and you'll get it in cash.

MILO. Why should this man be so generous?

ANDREW. Because he will have what fences never have - title to the jewels. I will see to it that in addition to the jewels, you also steal the receipts I got for them. All you have to do is hand them over together. Now what does my Insurance Company discover when it swings into action, antennae pulsing with suspicion? It discovers that someone impersonating Andrew Wyke sold the jewels for £90,000 cash. They've still got to pay me. Hard cheese. Think it over. Take your time. There's no hurry.

(A pause. MILO considers the proposition. ANDREW walks away from MILO, humming lightly to himself. He stops by a roll-a-penny wall game and plays to a successful conclusion. MILO paces up and down, indecisive. He suddenly turns and faces ANDREW)

MILO. Look, I know this sounds stupid, but... but well, have you had any experience - I mean, have you ever actually committed a crime before?

ANDREW. Only in the mind's eye, so to speak. For the purpose of my books. St. John Lord Merridew would have a pretty lean time of it if I didn't give him any crime to solve.

MILO. Who?

ANDREW. My detective, St. John Lord Merridew. Known to millions all over the civilized world. 'An ambulatory tun of port with the face of Father Christmas'. That's how I describe him. 'A classical scholar with a taste for good pipes and bad puns, but with a nose for smelling out evil, superior to anything, in the force'.

MILO. Oh yes, the police are always stupid in your kind of story, aren't they? They never solve anything. Only an amateur sleuth ever knows what's happening. But that is detective fiction. This is fact.

ANDREW. I am aware of the difference, Milo. I also know that insurance investigators are sharp as razors, and that's why, as they say in the Athenaeum, everything's got to be done Kosher and according to cocker.

MILO. I'm just saying there's a difference between writing and real life, that's all. And there's another thing. How do I know this thing isn't one big frame up?

ANDREW. Frame up?

MILO. Yes. That you really hate my association with your wife and would give five years of Olympian sexual athleticism to see me in jail. Once I'm clear of the house, an anonymous 'phone call to the police...

ANDREW. And be stuck with Marguerite for another bickering eternity? Bodystockings on the breakfast tray, false eyelashes in the wash basin, the bottles, the lotions, the unguents, the oils, the tribal record player and that ceaseless vapid yak. Oh yes, I could shop you to the police, nothing easier, but whatever for. Still, it's for you to evaluate, old boy.

MILO. Well I... I er...

ANDREW. If you don't trust me...

MILO. Oh, I trust you but...

ANDREW. It's a very simple proposition. You have an expensive woman and no money. It seems to me if you want to keep Marguerite there is only one thing you can do - you must steal those jewels.

MILO. Why don't you steal them and simply hand them over to me?

ANDREW. I should have thought that was obvious. The burglary has to look real. The house has actually to be broken into.

MILO. Well, why don't you break into it?

ANDREW. (Brooklyn accent) Hey, Milo baby, will you do me a favour. Leave this to me, huh? You know what I mean? Crime is my specialty. I've got such a great plan and I've got it all worked out to the last detail. You're the star, I'm just the producer.

MILO. £90,000?

ANDREW. (deliberately) £90,000 tax free. In cash. It would take a lot of Tindle Tours to make that kind of money. (they laugh together. MILO is convinced)

MILO. Alright, I'll do it. Where shall I break in? (MILO rushes for the stairs)

ANDREW. Hold your horses. Now the first thing you've got to do is disguise yourself.

MILO. What on earth for?

ANDREW. Supposing someone saw you climbing in.

MILO. Who? You're not overlooked.

ANDREW. Who knows? A dallying couple. A passing sheep rapist. And, dear boy, remember the clues we're to
28 leave for the police and the Insurance Company. We

don't want your footsteps in the flowerbeds, or your coat button snagged on the window-sill. Oh no, you must be disguised.

MILO. Alright, what do you suggest?

ANDREW. (ANDREW crosses to U.L. and brings a large hamper to D.L.) As Marguerite has assuredly told you, in younger days we were always dressing up in this house. What with amateur dramatics, and masquerades and costume balls, there was virtually no end to the concealment of identity.

MILO. She's never mentioned it.

ANDREW. No...? (a touch wistful) Well, it was all some years ago. (briskly) Anyway, let's see what we've got. (he opens the basket. He holds up the pieces of the burglar suit one by one and puts them on MILO). Item. A face mask, a flat cap, a striped jersey and bag marked Swag.

MILO. I thought the idea was that I was not to be taken as a burglar.

ANDREW. Fashions have changed you know.

MILO. Not quickly enough. It's asking for trouble.

(ANDREW puts the costume back and brings out a Ku Klux Klan outfit)

ANDREW. Ku Klux Klan invade country home. Fiery cross, flames on Salisbury plain. Police baffled.

MILO. Isn't it a trifle conspicuous for Wiltshire?

ANDREW. Yes, you may be right! (ANDREW holds up a monk's costume) Here is one of my favourites. How about Brother Lightfingers?

MILO. Oh, for God's sake...

(MILO shakes his head decisively)

ANDREW. Oh, come on. Let's make this a Gothic folly.
(Jesuit priest voice) Perhaps we shall never
know the identity of the cowled figure seen haunting
the grounds of the Manor House on the night of the
terrible murder. Even today, some locals claim to
hear the agonised screams of the victim echoing
around the chimney pots.

MILO. Murder? Anguished screams of the victim? What
are you talking about? It's a simple robbery we're
staging here, that's all.

(An uneasy pause)

ANDREW. (normal voice) Quite right, Milo. I was carried
away for a moment. I'm not sure I wasn't going to add
a crucified countess entombed in her bedroom, guarded
by a man eating sparrow-hawk.

MILO. Look here, Andrew, you probably think this is one
huge joke. But it's my freedom you're playing with.

ANDREW. I'm merely trying to bring a little romance into
modern crime, and incidentally into your life.

MILO. Marguerite will bring all the romance into my life
I need, thank you all the same.

ANDREW. Marguerite romantic? Marguerite couldn't have
got Johann Strauss to waltz.

MILO. Look, Andrew, these are great costumes, but
haven't you just got an old pair of wellies, a rain-
coat and a sock that I can pull over my head?

ANDREW. Old pair of wellies and a sock? How dreary!
That's the whole trouble with crime today. No
imagination. I mean you tell me, does your heart
beat any faster when you hear that a lorry load of
cigarettes has been knocked off in the Walworth
Road?

MILO. Not particularly.

ANDREW. Well of course not. Or that a 93 year old night watchman has had his silly interfering old skull split open with a lead pipe?

MILO. Of course not.

ANDREW. Well then, what's the matter with you? Where's your spunk? Let's give our crime the true sparkle of the thirties, a little amateur aristocratic quirkiness. Think of all that wonderful material. There's the ice dagger, the poison that leaves no trace, the Regie cigarette stubbed in the ash tray, charred violet note paper in the grate, Dusenberg tyre marks in the drive way, the gramophone record simulating conversation, the clutching hand from behind the arras, sinister orientals, twin brothers from Australia, "hi there cobber, hi there blue", where were you on the night of the 13th? I swear I didn't do it, Inspector, I'm innocent I tell you, innocent ...

MILO. God you've gone off like a fire-cracker!

ANDREW. And why not? We're on the brink of a great crime. Don't you feel the need to give your old arch-enemy Inspector Plodder of the Yard a run for his money? And you're the Star, you're the who-what-dun-it!

MILO. Well what about this? (He holds up Courtier's costume)

ANDREW. Ah! Monsieur Beaucaire. He's very good. Lots of beauty spots and wig powder to let fall all over the place. Or what about this? Little Bo Peep?

(ANDREW sings Little Bo Peep and dances about holding up the costume)

MILO. No.

ANDREW. Why not?

MILO. I haven't got the figure for it.

ANDREW. Are you quite sure? An indifferent figure shouldn't materially affect the execution of this crime.

MILO. Quite sure.

ANDREW. Well you are choosey, aren't you? There's not a great deal left.

(He pulls out a Clown's costume. Large pantaloons, waiter's dicky, tail coat)

We'll have to settle for Joey.

MILO. Wow!

ANDREW. Can't you see it all, the tinsel, the glitter, the lights, the liberty horses, the roar of the crowd, and Milo all the kiddies love you.

MILO. (happily) Alright! It seems the costume most appropriate to this scheme.

ANDREW. Well give me your coat I'll hang it up for you. We don't want the police to find any fibres of this beautiful suit.

(MILO takes off his jacket and gives it to ANDREW)

Oh and the shirt and trousers too.

MILO. What?

ANDREW. Oh yes, you know how clever they are in those laboratories of theirs. That's it. Don't be shy. Into your smalls. Oh I know a well brought up boy when I see one. Folds his pants at night.

(MILO gives him his carefully folded trousers. ANDREW runs up the stairs and with a sudden violent gesture, roughly throws the suit in the wardrobe, while MILO takes off his shirt and tie and shoes)

32

MILO. Shirt and shoes.

(MILO holds up his shirt, shoes and tie)

ANDREW. Very good, sir. The Quick Clean Valet Service always at your disposal, sir.

(He pushes them into the wardrobe, then watches MILO changing with great satisfaction)

(softly) Give a clown your finger and he'll take your hand.

MILO. What was that?

ANDREW. Just an old English Proverb I was thinking of.

(MILO sings to himself "On With the Motley" and ends it with "£90,000 tax free, in cash" as he dresses)

MILO. Ecco, Milo!

ANDREW. Bravissimo! Now all you need are the boots.

(MILO pulls a huge pair of boots from the basket)

MILO. Hey I could go skiing on these when I go to Italy.

ANDREW.   The clown is such a happy chap,
                 His nose is painted red,
                 His trousers baggy as can be,
                 A topper on his head.
                 He jumps around the circus ring,
                 And juggles for his bread,
                 Then comes the day he tries a trick,
                 And drops down ...

Come on do us a trick.

MILO. What sort of trick?

ANDREW. Oh I don't know. Trip up - fall on your arse.

MILO. Certainly not, I don't think that's a very good idea.

33

ANDREW. Well what about a bit of juggling then.

> (ANDREW takes two oranges from the drinks table
> and throws them to MILO. He then produces an
> umbrella from the basket and throws it to MILO who
> opens it and runs about the room and finally trips up
> on his boots)

MILO. Christ!

ANDREW. Sorry, dear boy. But you know the rule of the
circus. If at first you don't succeed...

MILO. Give up. Can we get on with this charade, please!

ANDREW. Of course. Yours to command. (he opens swag
bag) Here are the tools of your trade. One glass cutter
to break in with; a piece of putty for holding on to the
cut piece of glass so it doesn't clatter onto the floor
and awake the ravenous Doberman Pincher you suspect
lurks inside; and a stethoscope.

MILO. A stethoscope?

ANDREW. Safe breakers for the use of. The theory is you
tried to pick the lock by listening to the tumblers,
failed, and then employed gelignite.

MILO. (alarmed) Gelignite? I don't know anything about
gelignite.

ANDREW. I do. Leave that to me. Now what we want is
some supreme bizarre touch to crown the whole edifice
- say a signed photograph of Grock left impaled on a
splinter of glass.

MILO. A signed photograph of Grock. (angry) Why don't
you take a full page ad in The Times and tell them what
we're doing.

ANDREW. I was only trying to lighten Inspector Plodder's
day for him... If you don't like the idea...

MILO. (earnestly) There's no such animal as Inspector

Plodder outside of books. It'll be Inspector Early
Bird, or Superintendent No Stone Unturned. You can
bet your bottom dollar on that. And I can't walk in
this costume. These boots are ridiculous. (he
stumbles and starts to take them off)

ANDREW. Keep them on. Can't you see it all. Wiltshire
paralysed. The West Country in a ferment. Where
will Big Boot strike next?

MILO. But...

ANDREW. (reasonably) All these boots will tell the police
is that a true professional realised the flower beds
would carry footprints, and decided to disguise his
own perhaps a trifle eccentrically. Now are you
ready? Got everything? Glass cutter? Putty?

ANDREW.)
MILO.   )   The mask!

(ANDREW takes top hat and mask from basket)

ANDREW. Good. Now go through that door, round the
house and across the lawn. To your right you will
discover a shed. In it is a ladder. Bring the ladder
back and stand it against the house so you can break in
at the gallery.

MILO. Will you come out and hold it steady?

ANDREW. Certainly not. I don't want my footprints in
the flower beds.

MILO. I'm not very good at heights.

ANDREW. Improvise, ducky. Place one foot above the
other. It's called climbing.

MILO. OK.

ANDREW. Good luck.

(MILO bows and goes through the hall door. ANDREW

takes a length of flex and black box with gelignite,
black tape and detonator from desk drawer. After a
few minutes MILO appears at window U. L.)

ANDREW. (pause) For Christ's sake can't you keep
those bloody boots off my Busy Lizzies.

(MILO disappears and presently reappears with the
ladder which he places against the window and starts
to climb. ANDREW sits with his back to the window
and reacts to the noises he hears. As he attaches the
detonator to the flex he speaks in an old woman's
voice)

Puss, Puss, Puss, do you hear a noise Puss! Was
that a step on the stairs. No, it was just the wind.
You know Puss I sometimes think there's a curse on
this house. But you shouldn't pay any attention to me.
I'm just a silly old woman who is afraid of her own
shadow. (noise of glass cutter scoring window) What
was that Puss? Someone's prowling in the grounds.
We're all going to be murdered in our beds. No, no,
the front door's locked, and the window's too high, no
one can get into our snug little home.

(MILO drops pane of glass)

(exasperated) What are you doing now?

MILO. I dropped the glass.

(ANDREW groans theatrically. After a further struggle
MILO succeeds in climbing through the window, onto
the gallery)

Whew! What do I do with the putty?

(He indicates the putty)

ANDREW. (irritated) Stick it on the wall.

MILO. I can lose this at any rate. (puts mask on bureau)
Now for the safe!

ANDREW. No. Not straight away. You're not meant to
know where they are. Search around. Go into the
bedroom. Disturb a few things. Throw some clothes
on the floor - Marguerite's for choice... That's it.

(MILO goes into the bedroom and returns with a pile
of women's clothes which he puts neatly on the floor)

Don't pack 'em. Ravage 'em. Don't you know how
burglars leave a place?

(ANDREW takes a flying kick at the pile of his wife's
clothes - sending them flying all over the room)

Now try the wardrobe. Rumple the contents a little.
Actually that's enough. Those shirts were made for
me by Baget & Grub, chemise makers to monarchs.

(MILO throws the shirts out with relish)

MILO. Got to be thorough. It would be suspicious if the
burglar played favourites.

(ANDREW's socks and underwear follow, cascading out
all over the gallery)

ANDREW. Oh, it's a martyrdom. (shouting) Will you
stop that, Milo, and rifle that bureau immediately.

(Reluctantly MILO crosses to the bureau and tries a
drawer)

MILO. It's locked.

ANDREW. Of course it's bloody locked! Use your jemmy
on it.

MILO. I haven't got a jemmy. You didn't give me one.

ANDREW. (exasperated) Well, we'd better go and find
one, hadn't we?

(They tramp downstairs)

Honestly, Milo, you are the soppiest night interloper
I've ever met. I can't think what Marguerite sees in
you.

MILO. The sympathy and kindness of a kindred spirit,
actually.

ANDREW. It's like a Bengali tiger lying down with a Bush
Baby.

MILO. I know we're a damn sight happier than you are
with your ice maiden.

ANDREW. You probably take it more seriously, that's
all.

MILO. You have to be serious if you want to be in love.

ANDREW. You have to be serious about crime if you want
to afford to be in love. Now get cracking on that
bureau.

(MILO climbs the stairs. He starts work on the bureau
with the jemmy. After a pause the drawer yields and
he opens it)

MILO. There is a set of false teeth here. They look like a
man's.

ANDREW. (furious) Put them back at once.

MILO. Sorry. Your spares?

ANDREW. (pause) Come down at once.

(MILO comes down the stairs and crosses to ANDREW
who has plugged the flex into a light switch U. stage
left)

Keep your feet off the flex. Right, stand by for count
down 5 - 4 - 3 - 2 - 1. Contact!

(Noise of explosion and puff of smoke from safe)

MILO. There she blows. Ah! It's hot.

ANDREW. You've got gloves on! - Get in there!

(MILO rummages in the safe and finds a large jewel
box. He examines it carefully, occasionally shaking
it gently)

What the hell are you shaking it for? It's a jewel box,
not a maracca.

MILO. I thought it might have some secret catch on it.
It's locked, you see.

ANDREW. Well, smash it open. Jesus! You've all the
killer instinct of a twenty year old Sealyham.

(MILO attacks the box with his jemmy)

MILO. It's such a pretty box - it seems such a waste.

(The box opens to reveal its precious contents. MILO
stands entranced letting the jewels flash and sparkle
through his fingers)

Dear God!

ANDREW. Ah! Moses looks upon the promised land.

(MILO sits at base of stairs)

MILO. They're very beautiful. Look at this ruby necklace?

ANDREW. That we got on our honeymoon.

MILO. It's fantastic.

ANDREW. I never cared for it myself. I always thought
it made Marguerite look like a blood sacrifice.

MILO. I'd like my father to be here now. Poor blighter,
he had no idea what it was all about... sitting there
every night hunched up over those watches like a little

old gnome, squinting his eyesight away, and for what -
to give me an education at a second-rate public school.
I suppose he thought he had to do it - that he owed it
to me and the brave new Anglo-Saxon world he'd
adopted. Poor old bugger.

ANDREW. Here, put them in your pocket for a start.
I'll get you the receipts in a moment. Now! This is
the fun bit. It's the moment when the householder, his
attention attracted by the sound of the explosion,
surprises his burglar. In the ensuing struggle, the house
is sacked.

MILO. Why is it necessary for you to surprise me at all?

ANDREW. Because if I've seen you at close quarters, I
can always describe you to the police...

(MILO reacts as if hit)

MILO. Now look here...

ANDREW. ...wrongly. (INSPECTOR's voice) Did you
manage to get a good look at the intruder's face, sir?
(normal voice) Yes, Inspector, I did. It may just have
been a trick of the light, but his face didn't look wholly
human. If you can imagine a kind of prognathic stoat,
fringed about with lilac coloured hair, and seemingly
covered in a sort of boot polish...

MILO. (patiently) I understand. How much sacking do you
want done?

ANDREW. A decent bit, I think, a few chairs on their
backs, some china ornaments put to the sword. You
know - convincing but not Carthaginian.

(MILO carefully turns a chair over and leans a small
table against the sofa. He takes a china ornament and
stands it upright on the floor. ANDREW watches
impatiently)

Surely you don't call that convincing?

(ANDREW throws over another table, spills the contents of a drawer, and turns books out of his bookcase)

That's better. Let the encyclopaedias fly like autumn leaves. Let the contents of the drawers be scattered to the four winds!

(MILO throws papers into the air in a great cloud)

Ah! A super snowstorm. That's very good. We'll let my accountants sort that lot out later. You know I never liked Saltglaze. I can't think why Marguerite is devoted to it. (he picks a china ornament off the mantelpiece and hurls it across the room) Oh it's coming along nicely, but it still doesn't look right. Come on, let's see what accident does to artifice. (ANDREW seizes MILO and wrestles him round the room, overturning things as they go. MILO, apart from being the shorter, is much hampered by his big boots and floppy clown's clothing, so that ANDREW is able to pummel him severely)

MILO. You're bigger than I am. It's not fair.

ANDREW. Nonsense. You're the underdog, aren't you? You've got the support of the crowd.

MILO. A good big 'un will always lick a good little 'un.

ANDREW. The bigger they are the harder they fall.

(MILO receives a particularly hard blow)

MILO. Here, steady on, old man!

ANDREW. They never come back. (he pushes MILO over the fender into the fireplace)

MILO. Christ! That hurt!

(ANDREW helps him up)

ANDREW. Come on, back into the ring. Don't despair. This fight is fixed. It's about now that I take a dive.

41

This is where you lay me out cold.

MILO. What? For real?

ANDREW. Naturally. When the police come I must be able to show them a real bump.

(MILO smiles weakly)

I thought you'd like this bit.

(MILO tentatively moves towards a lamp)

MILO. What shall I use?

ANDREW. Not my opaline if you don't mind.

(MILO picks up the brass poker)

MILO. This is it. The poker, the original blunt instrument. (he beats logs viciously)

(ANDREW eyes the poker apprehensively)

ANDREW. Steady on, Milo. Don't get carried away.

MILO. Well, I'm doing my best.

ANDREW. We are not talking about a murder weapon. We are discussing an object from which I receive, in the classic formula, a glancing blow which renders me temporarily unconscious.

MILO. Such as?

ANDREW. Well I don't know exactly... Frankly I'm rather off this blow business now I've seen you in action. Perhaps we could think of a device which will raise a lump without actually cracking the cranium. Yes, that's it. Now what would those fathers of the scientific detective story, R. Austin Freeman, or Arthur B. Reeve have come up with?

MILO. Huh?

ANDREW. You know. The Red Thumb Mark 1907. The Silent Bullet 1912.

MILO. (trapped into joining in) How about a bee sting projected into the scalp with a blow pipe.

ANDREW. Oh, Milo, that's absolutely brilliant. Do you have such sting, pipe, or bee?

MILO. Well... no.

ANDREW. No. Still seven out of ten for trying. I know, you can always tie me up and gag me and leave me to be found by the cleaning woman. (CHARLADY's voice) Lawks, Mr. Wyke, what are you doing all trussed up like a turkey cock?

(ANDREW mimes being tied up and gagged and trying to get the Charlady to untie him)

Mmmmmmmmmmmmmm...Mmmmmmmmmmmmm... Mmmmmmmmmmmmmm... (CHARLADY's voice) Trying out something for one of them creepy books of yours, are you, sir? Well, don't mind me. I won't disturb you. I'll just get on with my dusting.

MILO. (patiently) If I don't knock you out, how do I manage to tie you up?

ANDREW. (normal voice) That's a very good question. I know. You could hold a gun on me.

MILO. We professional burglars don't like firearms much.

ANDREW. But, as you're a rank amateur you can conquer your scruples.

(ANDREW produces a gun from the desk drawer)

Here. How about this? Don't you think its wicked looking blue barrel is just the thing.

MILO. Is it loaded?

ANDREW. Naturally. What use would it be otherwise?
And I think it should go off a couple of times in the
struggle.

MILO. Why?

ANDREW. It would add credence to my story of your
holding a gun on me. Hearing a noise and fearing
burglars, I took my revolver and went to investigate.
You attacked me. In the struggle it went off. Being
an old fraidy cat householder, I allowed brutish you
to take possession of it. You then held it on me while
you tied me up. Right?

MILO. I suppose so.

ANDREW. Uninventive but believable. Now then, what to
sacrifice? What do you say to the demolition of that
gaudy Swansea puzzle jug? The gloriously witty idea
is that when you tip it up the liquid pours out of a hole
in the back, and not through the spout.

MILO. A bit obvious, really.

ANDREW. Exactly! Obvious and ugly. Let us expose
its shortcomings.

(ANDREW draws a bead on it, then lowers the gun)

On the other hand, the creme brule colouring lends it
an attractive solidity I should miss. Now how about
that giant Staffordshire mug with the inscription on it?
What does it say?

(MILO moves a little towards it and reads it out)

MILO. (reading) In the real cabinet of friendship everyone
helped his neighbour and said to his brother be of good
cheer.

ANDREW. Proletarian pomposity!

(ANDREW suddenly raises his gun and fires, shattering

the jug. MILO turns in surprise, as he realises the
bullet must have passed reasonably close to his head)

You might have said good shot.

MILO. Good shot.

ANDREW. (insouciant) It's nothing.

(ANDREW looks around him. His eye falls on a china
figurine poised on the banister rail above him. He
takes aim)

Down with all deviationist, reactionary Dresden
Shepherdesses.

(He shoots and the Dresden Shepherdess flies into pieces)

MILO. Bravo!

ANDREW. What fun this is! Did you ever know Charlie
Begby?

MILO. I don't think so.

ANDREW. Terribly funny fellow. I once saw him bag three
brace of duck with one shot.

MILO. No!

ANDREW. Yes. Three brace with one shot! The only
trouble was, they were china ducks on his aunty's
drawing room wall. I said "oh Charlie you can't do
that, it's the close season". (he presses a button on
the desk and the sailor laughs) I told you, he always
laughs at my jokes.

(MILO laughs. ANDREW's mood changes abruptly)

It's not really all that funny. There's an open season
on some creatures all the year round.

(ANDREW turns the gun on MILO)

Seducers and wife stealers for example.

MILO. (nervous) Only in Italian opera surely.

ANDREW. (hard) You should know. It's your country of
   origin, is it not?

MILO. No. I was actually born here in England.

ANDREW. Were you now. Dear old cradle-of-the-
   parliamentary-system-who-screws-my-wife-merits-
   a-large-pink-gin-England?

MILO. Sense-of-humour-fair-trail-England, I mean.

ANDREW. That's the way a foreigner talks. In private he
   thinks, filthy wet country, ugly red cold men who don't
   know how to treat women.

MILO. What's brought all this on? What are you doing
   with that gun?

ANDREW. Pretty obviously pointing it at you.

MILO. For God's sake, why?

ANDREW. (slowly, Italian accent) Because I'm going to
   kill you.

MILO. You're going to... (laughs nervously) Oh Jesus!
   I suppose this is some sort of game.

ANDREW. Yes. We've been playing it all evening. It's
   called 'You're going to die and no-one will suspect
   murder'.

(A pause. MILO considers his position)

MILO. You mean all this steal my wife's jewels stuff was
   just a...

ANDREW. Of course! I invited you here to set up the
   circumstances of your own death. The break in, the
   disguise, the jewels in your pocket, the householder

46

aroused, the gun going off in the struggle and then the final fatal shot. I might even get a commendation from the police, for "having a go".

MILO. For God's sake, Andrew, knock it off!

ANDREW. Can you find a flaw in it?

MILO. (beginning to feel desperate) Marguerite! They'll trace the connection between me and Marguerite. They'll know that's why you did it.

ANDREW. I am quite entitled to tackle a man wearing a mask plundering my house in the middle of the night. How was I expected to know who you were? Oh no, the law will have every sympathy with me. Property has always been more highly regarded than people in England. Even Marguerite will assume you were just an adventurer who only loved her for her jewels - a petty sneak thief who found larceny less burdensome than marriage. You really are a dead duck, aren't you? Not a moral or romantic attitude left.

MILO. I believe you are serious.

ANDREW. I'm not afraid of killing you, if that's what you mean.

MILO. You've got to be. Mortally afraid for your soul.

ANDREW. I didn't think the Jews believed in hell.

MILO. We believe in not playing games with life.

ANDREW. Ha! Wit in the face of adversity. You've learnt something from the English. Well here's something else to learn. A sporting chance. Why don't you run for it?

MILO. And give you the chance to shoot me down in cold blood?

ANDREW. In hot blood you mean. I'm going to shoot you down in cold blood anyway.

(MILO tries to run but falls over his boots)

MILO. Look, stop pointing that gun at me...I hate guns...
please...this is sick.

ANDREW. You should be flattered by the honour I'm doing
you - to take your life lightheartedly - to make your
death the centre piece of an arranged bit of fun. To put
it another way, your demise will recreate a noble mind.

MILO. This is where I came in.

ANDREW. And where you go out, I'm afraid. The only
question to be decided is where the police shall find
you. Sprawled over the desk like countless colonels
in countless studies? Or propped up in the log basket
like a rag doll? Which do you think? Early Agatha
Christie or middle Nicholas Blake?

MILO. For Christ's sake, Andrew, this is not a detective
story, this is real life. You are talking of doing a
real murder. Of killing a real man - don't you
understand?

ANDREW. Perhaps I shouldn't do it with a gun at all.
Perhaps I should shove the ham knife into you, and
leave you face down in the middle of the room -
(melodramatic voice) - your blood staining the flag-
stones a deep carmine.

(MILO shudders)

MILO. Oh God!

ANDREW. Or best of all, how about a real 1930's murder
weapon - the mashie niblick. I've got one in my golf
bag.

(ANDREW fetches the golf club from the hall. MILO
dives for the telephone but is too late)

You would be discovered in the fireplace, I think in a
fair old mess. (dramatic voice) The body lay on its
back, its limbs grotesquely splayed like a broken

puppet. The whole head had been pulped as if by some
superhuman force. (INSPECTOR's voice) "My God"
breathed the Inspector, blenching. "Thompson, you'd
better get a tarpaulin... Excuse me sir, but was all
this violence strictly necessary?" (own voice) I'm
sorry Inspector. It was when I saw him handling my
wife's nightdresses. I must have completely lost
control of myself. (INSPECTOR's voice) "That's
quite alright sir. Don't get excited. I quite understand." (ANDREW throws down golf club) No. I
don't like it. I think the scene the police find is
simply this. After the fight you flee up the stairs to
regain your ladder. I catch you on the landing and in
the renewed struggle I shoot you. Nothing succeeds
like simplicity, don't you agree, Milo? Now then,
some of my own finger prints on my own revolver.
(ANDREW takes his glove off and holds the gun in his
naked hand) On your feet, up!

(ANDREW forces MILO to mount the stairs by shoving
the gun in his back. MILO gives a sudden spasmodic
shudder)

Did you know that Charles I put on two shirts the
morning of his execution? "If I tremble with cold,"
he said, "my enemies will say it was from fear; I
will not expose myself to such reproaches". You
must also attempt dignity as you mount the steps to the
scaffold.

(MILO demurs and sinks to his knees near the top step)

MILO. (terrified and pleading) But why, Andrew? Why?

ANDREW. Don't snivel. You can't think it'll gain you mercy.

MILO. I must know why!

ANDREW. I'm amazed you have to ask. But since you do,
    it's perfectly simple. I hate you. I hate your smarmy,
    good looking Latin face and your easy manner. I'll
    bet you're easy in a ski lodge, and easy on a yacht,
    and easy on a beach. I'll bet you a pound to a penny,

49

that you wear a gold charm round your neck, and that your chest is hairy and in summer matted with sun oil. I hate you because you are a mock humble, jewelled, shot cuff-link sponger, a world is my oysterer, a seducer of silly women, and a king among marsh-mallow snakes. I hate you because you are a culling spick. A wop - a not one of me. Come, little man, did you really believe I would give up my wife and jewels to you? That I would make myself that ridiculous?

MILO. Why not? You're not in love with her.

ANDREW. She's mine whether I love her or not. I found her, I've kept you. I am familiar with her. And once, she was in love with me.

MILO. And now she's in love with me, and the dog in the manger won't let go. (tries to attack him) The mad dog in the manger who should be put down for every-one's sake.

ANDREW. (deadly) And you are a young man, dressed as a clown about to be murdered. Put the mask on, Milo. (a pause)

MILO. No please.

(ANDREW reaches up and lifts the clown mask off the newel post)

ANDREW. Put it on!

(MILO takes the mask and fumbles it onto his face)

Excellent. Farewell Punchinello!

(ANDREW lifts the pistol to MILO's head. MILO is shaking with fear)

MILO. (high falsetto) Please...

(ANDREW slowly pulls the trigger. MILO falls

backwards down the stairs and lies still. ANDREW walks past him, pausing to peer closely to see whether there is any sign of life. He lifts the lolling head and lets it thump back, carelessly, onto the stairs. Satisfied that he has done his work well, he straightens up, and smiles to himself)

ANDREW. Game and set, I believe.

Slow Curtain

ACT TWO

(The curtain rises to the sound of the slow movement
of Beethoven's Seventh Symphony which is playing on
a record player. ANDREW enters from kitchen with
a tray containing a large pot of caviare, toast, wedge
of lemon, a bottle of champagne and glass. He puts
tray on desk and stands conducting the music. The
Movement comes to an end. ANDREW crosses to
record player and turns over the record. He returns
to desk and starts to eat.

The telephone rings)

ANDREW. Hullo... Yes, Hawkins, where are you? What?
  Well, you should have checked the times of the trains...
  I've had to get my own supper for the third time running
  ... Yes, yes, I daresay, but you know how helpless I
  am without you and Mrs. H. Man cannot live on Baked
  Beans alone, you know... Alright... Alright, tomorrow
  morning. But first thing, mind you.

  (ANDREW continues eating for some moments. The front
  doorbell rings. After a slight pause ANDREW goes to
  answer it)

DOPPLER. (off stage in hall) Good evening, sir.

ANDREW. Evening.

DOPPLER. Mr. Wyke.

ANDREW. Yes?

DOPPLER. My name is Inspector Doppler, sir. Detective
Inspector Doppler. Of the Wiltshire County
Constabulary. I'm sorry to be calling so late. May I
have a few words with you on a very important matter?

(ANDREW enters, followed by INSPECTOR DOPPLER,
a heavily built, tallish man of about 50. His hair is
balding, and he wears cheap round spectacles on his
fleshy nose, above a greying moustache. His clothes,
dark rumpled suit, under a half-open light coloured
mackintosh occasion no surprise, nor does his pork
pie hat)

ANDREW. The Wiltshire County Constabulary you say?
(turning off music) Come in. Always pleased to see
the police.

DOPPLER. Can't say the same about everyone, sir. Most
people seem to have what you might call an allergy to
us.

ANDREW. Would you join me in a brandy, Inspector? Or
are you going to tell me you don't drink on duty?

DOPPLER. Oh no, sir. I always drink on duty. I can't
afford to in my own time.

(DOPPLER sits Centre)

ANDREW. (handing the INSPECTOR a brandy) Well, what
can I do for you, Inspector?

DOPPLER. I'm investigating a disappearance, sir.

ANDREW. Disappearance?

DOPPLER. Yes, sir. Of a Mr. Milo Tindle. Do you know
him, sir?

ANDREW. Yes, that's the chap who's taken Laundry
Cottage.

DOPPLER. He walked out of his cottage on Friday night and hasn't been seen since.

ANDREW. Great Scott.

DOPPLER. Do you know this gentleman well, sir?

ANDREW. Vaguely. He came to the house once or twice. How can I help you?

DOPPLER. When did you last see Mr. Tindle, sir?

ANDREW. Oh, months ago. I can't exactly remember. As I told you, he wasn't a close friend; rather more an acquaintance.

DOPPLER. Really, sir. That doesn't quite accord with our information. In fact, he told Jack Benn, the Licensee of the White Lion he was coming to see you, two nights ago.

ANDREW. Publicans are notorious opponents of exactitude, Inspector. Vinous gossip is their stock in trade. In particular, I've always found that Jack Benn's observations need constant correction.

DOPPLER. Really, sir. I was wondering if you could correct something else for me.

ANDREW. What's that?

DOPPLER. The impression gained by a man who happened to be passing your house two nights ago, that a fierce struggle was taking place in here.

ANDREW. Does it look like it?

DOPPLER. And that shots were fired?

ANDREW. (uncertainly) Shots?

DOPPLER. Three, our man thinks.

ANDREW. A car backfiring?

57

DOPPLER. No, sir. These were shots. From a gun. Our man is positive.

ANDREW. May I ask why you took two days to call round and ask me about all this?

DOPPLER. Well, sir, things take longer to check out than you think. We like to be certain of our facts before troubling a gentleman like yourself.

ANDREW. Facts? What facts?

DOPPLER. After our informant reported the incident, we did a spot of checking in the village, and as I say Mr. Benn was very helpful.

ANDREW. There's an upright citizen, then.

DOPPLER. Quite so, sir.

ANDREW. If there were more like him...

DOPPLER. He told us that Mr. Tindle popped into the pub Friday evening for a quick one, and said he was just on his way up to you. Well, what with him being a newcomer to these parts and all, we thought we'd better have a word with him, and see if he could throw any light on the subject. But as I previously indicated he seems to have disappeared, sir.

ANDREW. But what's that got to do with me?

DOPPLER. He wasn't at his cottage all of Saturday, nor all today. We must have called half a dozen times.

ANDREW. By Jove, Merridew would have been proud of you. Now Inspector, if that's all you have to say...

DOPPLER. When we stepped inside Mr. Tindle's cottage to make sure he'd come to no harm, we found this note, sir. (reading) "Urgent we talk. Come Friday night eight o'clock. Wyke." May I ask whether this is your hand-writing, sir?

(DOPPLER shows him the note. ANDREW tries to retain it, but DOPPLER takes it back)

ANDREW. (trapped) Yes. It's mine alright.

DOPPLER. So Mr. Tindle was here?

ANDREW. Yes. The Potman spoke sooth.

DOPPLER. Perhaps you wouldn't mind answering my original question now, sir.

ANDREW. Which one?

DOPPLER. Was there a struggle here two nights ago?

ANDREW. In a manner of speaking, yes. It was a game we were playing.

DOPPLER. A game? What kind of game?

ANDREW. It's rather difficult to explain. It's called Burglary.

DOPPLER. Please don't joke, sir.

ANDREW. Isn't it about time you told me I don't know the seriousness of my own position?

DOPPLER. A man comes here, there is a fight. Shots are heard. He disappears. What would you make of that if you were me?

ANDREW. An open and shut case. But things are not always what they seem Inspector. In the case of "The Drowned Dummy" my man, Merridew, once proved by a phonetic mis-spelling the forgery of a document allegedly written by a deaf mute.

DOPPLER. I'm waiting for an explanation.

ANDREW. Tindle arrived at eight and left about an hour and a half later. I haven't seen him since.

DOPPLER. And nor has anyone else, sir.

ANDREW. This is absurd. Are you suggesting that I killed Tindle?

DOPPLER. Killed Tindle, sir. I never mentioned kill.

ANDREW. Oh really! You can't pull that old one on me.

(Joke INSPECTOR's voice)

Garotted, sir? Might I ask how you knew that her ladyship was garotted?

(Normal voice)

Surely you told me so Inspector.

(Inspector's voice)

No, sir. I never mentioned it.

DOPPLER. I'm sorry you find us so comic, sir. On the whole what we do is necessary.

ANDREW. "You're just doing your job,", that's the over-worked phrase, isn't it?

DOPPLER. Possibly, sir. Your wife and Mr. Tindle have been associating closely for some time.

ANDREW. Oh, so you know about that, do you. I suppose you can't keep anything quiet in a small village.

DOPPLER. Perfectly true, sir.

ANDREW. You aren't suggesting a crime passionel, I hope, Inspector - not over Marguerite. It would be like knifing somebody for a table-spoonful of Co-operative White blancmange.

DOPPLER. I'm very partial to blancmange, sir. I find it a great standby.

ANDREW. (oratorically) All of you had either means, motive or opportunity, said Inspector Doppler as he thoughtfully digested another spoonful of his favourite pud. But only one of you had all three.

DOPPLER. Exactly so, sir! That person is you.

ANDREW. Forgive me, Inspector, I suppose I'd better tell you what happened.

DOPPLER. Yes.

ANDREW. Want a bribe to believe it?

DOPPLER. I'll have another drink.

ANDREW. As you seem to know, Tindle was having an affair with my wife. Now, I'm one of that rare breed of men who genuinely don't mind losing gracefully to a gent who's playing by the same rules. But to be worsted by a flash crypto Italian lover, who mistakes my boredom for impotence and my provocative energy for narcissism is too much. It's like starting every game love-30 down, and the Umpire against you.

DOPPLER. You mean you couldn't bring yourself to accept the situation, sir. Is that what you're saying?

ANDREW. I think what infuriated me most was the things he said about me - things that Marguerite repeated to me. I mean no man likes to listen to the other man's witticisms when he's trying to choke down his late night Ovaltine.

DOPPLER. What sort of things, sir?

ANDREW. Oh you know, smarmy, deceitful things which any lover can make about any husband. It's just too easy for them with a captive audience groggy on rediscovered youth and penis envy. (pause) It's not really playing the game.

DOPPLER. You seem to regard marriage as a game, sir.

ANDREW. Not marriage, Inspector. Sex. Sex is the game with marriage the penalty. Round the board we jog towards each futile anniversary. Pass go. Collect 200 rows, 200 silence, 200 scars in the deep places. it's just as well that I don't lack for amorous adventure. Finlandia provides.

DOPPLER. Are you trying to tell me that because of your indifference to your wife, you had no motive for killing Mr. Tindle?

ANDREW. I'm simply saying that in common with most men I want to have my cookie and ignore it.

DOPPLER. Well, sir. I must say you're very frank.

ANDREW. Disarmingly so, I hope.

DOPPLER. Please go on.

ANDREW. As I say. I thought I'd teach Mr. Tindle a lesson for his presumption. In a curious way, some of his remarks which Marguerite repeated to me, led me to believe that he was worth taking a little trouble with - even perhaps worth getting to know. Now, the shortest way to a man's heart is humiliation. You soon find out what he's made of.

DOPPLER. So you invited him here and humiliated him?

ANDREW. I did indeed. I took a leaf out of the book of certain 18th century secret societies. They knew to a nicety how to determine whether someone was worthy to be included amongst their number and also how to humiliate him in the process. I refer of course to the initiation ceremony.

DOPPLER. Would it be something like bullying a new boy at school?

ANDREW. Not unlike, but the victim had the choice of refusal. When Count Cagliastro, the noted magician, sought admission to one such society, he was asked whether he was prepared to die for it, if need be. He said he was. He was then sentenced to death, blind-

folded and a pistol containing powder but no shot
placed against his temple and discharged.

DOPPLER. And you did this to Mr. Tindle?

ANDREW. More or less. I invited Milo here and suggested
to him that as my wife had expensive tastes and he was
virtually a pauper, the only course open for him was to
steal some valuable jewels which I had in the safe.

DOPPLER. And he agreed to this?

ANDREW. With alacrity. I persuaded him to get out of his
clothes and to dress as Grock, in which ludicrous disguise he broke into the house and blew open the safe.
He then pocketed the jewels, struggled, convincingly,
round this room and was about to make off, when I
turned nasty and revealed the purpose of the evening.
This, of course, was that I had manoeuvred him into a
position where by pretending to mistake him for a
burglar, I could, as the outraged householder,
legitimately shoot him as he raced away up the stairs.
By the time the police arrived I would be standing in my
night attire innocent, bewildered and aggrieved. And
as you well know, Inspector, there's no liar in Britain,
however unconvincing, more likely to be believed than
an owner occupier standing with his hair ruffled in
front of his own fireplace, wearing striped Viyella
pyjamas under a camel Jaeger dressing gown.

DOPPLER. What was Mr. Tindle's reaction to all this?

ANDREW. It was electrifying! He swallowed my story hook,
line and sinker. He fell on his knees, pleaded for his
life, but I was implacable. I put the gun against his
head and shot him with a blank cartridge. He fainted
dead away. It was most gratifying.

DOPPLER. Gratifying or not, sir. Mr. Tindle must have
been put in fear for his life. Such action invites a
grave charge of assault.

ANDREW. Well, I suppose that's marginally better than

the murder charge you were contemplating a few minutes ago.

DOPPLER. I still am contemplating it, sir.

ANDREW. Oh come now, Inspector. I've told you what happened. After a few minutes, Mr. Tindle recovered his senses, realised shrewdly that he wasn't dead after all and went off home.

DOPPLER. (shaking his head in disbelief) Just like that?

ANDREW. Well, he needed a glass or two of cognac to get the parts working. I mean, wouldn't you?

DOPPLER. I doubt whether I would have survived completely undamaged, sir. The whole thing sounds like the most irresponsible trick.

ANDREW. Irresponsible? It was quite the contrary. I was upholding the sanctity of marriage. That's more than most people are prepared to do these days. By this action I was clearly stating "Marriage isn't dead. It's alive and well and living in Wiltshire".

DOPPLER. Tell me, did Mr. Tindle say anything when he left?

ANDREW. No. He seemed speechless. (laughs) He just lurched off.

DOPPLER. I'm sorry you appear to find all this so funny, Mr. Wyke. We may not take quite the same attitude.

ANDREW. Look, why don't you see this from my point of view. In a sense, Milo was a burglar. He was stealing my wife.

DOPPLER. So you tortured him?

ANDREW. (exploding) Don't you see. It was a game!

DOPPLER. A game?

ANDREW. A bloody game, yes!

DOPPLER. It sounds rather sad, sir - like a child not growing up.

ANDREW. What's so sad about a child playing, eh!

DOPPLER. Nothing, sir - if you're a child.

ANDREW. Let me tell you, Inspector. I have played games of such complexity that Jung and Einstein would have been honoured to have been asked to participate in them. Games of construction and games of destruction. Games of hazard, and games of callidity. Games of deductive logic, inductive logic, semantics, colour association, mathematics, hypnosis and prestidigitation. I have achieved leaps of the mind and leaps of the psyche unknown in ordinary human relationships. And I've had a great deal of not wholly innocent fun.

DOPPLER. And now, sir, you have achieved murder.

ANDREW. No!

DOPPLER. I believe so, sir.

ANDREW. No!'.

DOPPLER. Would you mind if I looked around?

ANDREW. Go ahead. Crawl about the floor on hands and knees. Get your envelope out and imprison hairs. Gather ye blunt instruments while ye may.

(DOPPLER rises and starts to examine the room)

(slowly) I ask myself, if I wanted to conceal

(DOPPLER shakes the sailor on his passage round the room)

Milo, where would I put him? In the cellar? Too traditional! In the water tank?... Too poisonous! In the linen chest?... Too aromatic! In the furnace? ... Too residual! In the herbaceous border?... Too ossiferous! In the...   65

DOPPLER. Excuse me, sir, but these holes in the wall here and here. They look like bullet holes.

ANDREW. (slowly) Quite right, Inspector. So they are.

DOPPLER. I understand you to say, sir, that you used a blank.

ANDREW. Two live bullets to set up the trick. One blank to complete it. I had to persuade Tindle I was in earnest. After all, there's really no point in playing a game unless you play it to the hilt.

DOPPLER. I see, sir. One blank. I'd like you to show me where Mr. Tindle was when you killed him.

ANDREW. Pretended to kill him you mean.

DOPPLER. Quite so, sir. Show me, please, exactly where he was when the bullet hit him.

ANDREW. You do realise of course, there wasn't a real bullet.

DOPPLER. (sceptically) Very well, sir. Show me where he was when the blank cartridge was fired.

(ANDREW mounts the stairs followed by the Inspector)

ANDREW. He was standing, kneeling, crouching about here. He fainted and fell down the stairs. Bang!

(DOPPLER passes ANDREW)

DOPPLER. I see. About here you say, sir?

ANDREW. Towards me. Come on. Come on. Stop.

DOPPLER. Were you close to Mr. Tindle when you fired the gun?

ANDREW. Very. I was standing over him in fact, with the gun pressed against his head. The actual feel of the gun

coupled with the noise of the explosion was what did
the trick. (DOPPLER scrutinizes the staircase)
Inspector, I'd like to facilitate your work in every way.
Could I interest you in a magnifying glass? No?
(DOPPLER bends down to examine the staircase, then
the banisters, suddenly he rubs a finger on them, and
straightens up, wiping them on his handkerchief)

DOPPLER. Joke blood, sir?

ANDREW. (nervous) I'm not quite sure I follow, Inspector.

DOPPLER. This here on the banisters. It's dried blood.

ANDREW. Blood? Where?

DOPPLER. Here in the angle of the banister - (DOPPLER
scrapes some dried blood into an envelope)

(Warily ANDREW crosses to the stairs. He examines
the banisters and slowly straightens up. His expression
is confused and fearful)

Don't touch it, sir! Oh, look sir, here's some more.
Someone's been rubbing at the carpet. Do you see,
sir? There, deep in the pile that's blood, sir. Oh!
It's still damp. Could you explain how it got there,
sir?

ANDREW. I have no idea, Milo... er... he was a little
burnt... You must believe me!

DOPPLER. Why should I, sir?

ANDREW. But it's impossible, it was only a game.

DOPPLER. A game, sir? With real bullets and real blood?

ANDREW. (gabbling) There's the hole cut in the pane of
glass with the diamond cutter... and there are the
marks of the ladder on the sill outside... and if you
look down you'll see the imprint of the other end of the

ladder and of size twenty eight shoes or whatever they were, still there in the flowerbed and this is the bureau that he broke open... (DOPPLER descends the stairs)

DOPPLER. (hard) Thank you, sir, but I don't require a conducted tour. Over the years my eyes have been adequately trained to see things for themselves.

ANDREW. I'm sure they have, Inspector. I only meant to point out facts which would help substantiate my story. And that's the safe we blew open...

DOPPLER. Where are the jewels now, sir?

ANDREW. I put them in the bank yesterday.

DOPPLER. On a Saturday?

ANDREW. Yes, Inspector, on a Saturday. I went to Salisbury and I put them in the night safe. I felt they'd be better off there. I mean, anyone could break in and steal them.

DOPPLER. How provident, sir.

ANDREW. And look down the corridor, you'll see the dressing up basket...

(DOPPLER turns away and looks out of the window, over the garden)

DOPPLER. You didn't point out that mound of earth in the garden, did you, sir?

(ANDREW joins DOPPLER at the window)

ANDREW. Mound of earth? What mound of earth?

DOPPLER. Over there - by the far wall. In the shadow of that yew tree. Would you say it had been freshly dug, sir?

ANDREW. (shouting) How the hell should I know. It's probably something the gardener's doing. A new flowerbed I think he said.

DOPPLER. A flowerbed under a yew tree, sir?

ANDREW. (shouting) I've already told you I don't know.
Why don't you ask him yourself? He's probably out
there somewhere maundering around on his mole-
skinned knees aching for an opportunity to slander his
employer.

DOPPLER. Funny, sir. I've always found gardeners make
excellent witnesses. Slow, methodical, positive.

ANDREW. Inspector, I've had just about enough of this
farce. Go and dig the damned thing up, if you want to.

DOPPLER. Oh, we shall, sir. Don't worry.

ANDREW. (persuasive) Look, do you really think that I'd
bury Tindle in the garden, and leave all that newly
turned earth for everyone to find?

DOPPLER. If you weren't expecting us, sir, yes. In a
couple of weeks, with some bulbs or a little grass seed,
it would be difficult to tell it had ever been disturbed.
We in the police know just how fond murderers are of
their back gardens, sir.

ANDREW. (attempts a laugh) You're nearer a killer's
heart in a garden than anywhere else on earth, eh?

DOPPLER. Except a bedroom, sir. I think you'll find
that's still favourite.

(DOPPLER starts rummaging in the wardrobe)

Tch! Tch! Tch! What a way to keep your clothes! All
screwed up at the back of your wardrobe. Why should
you do that, I wonder.

(He holds up Milo's shirt)

That's an interesting monogram. I. W. No, I've got

it the wrong way up - M. T.

ANDREW. Let me see that.

DOPPLER. (reading) Made by Owen & Smith of Percy Street. 16.8.69 for Mr. Milo Tindle. Tell me something, sir.

(ANDREW seizes the shirt and stares at it in horror, unable to speak. DOPPLER holds up the jacket and carefully reads the name in the inside pocket)

When Mr. Tindle lurched off as you put it, did he lurch naked?

ANDREW. (in great distress) Believe me, Inspector. I have no idea how those clothes got there.

DOPPLER. Didn't you tell me that Mr. Tindle stripped off here the other night to disguise himself as a clown?

ANDREW. Yes, that's right.

DOPPLER. Another part of the humiliation process, I suppose?

ANDREW. But he changed back before he left. I mean, you can't really see him walking through the village dressed as a clown, can you?

DOPPLER. No, sir, I can't. Which makes the appearance of his clothes here all the more significant.

ANDREW. It's all so difficult...

DOPPLER. On the contrary, sir, I think it's all very simple. I think you started this as a game, exactly as you say you did, in order to play a diabolical trick on Mr. Tindle but that it went wrong. Your third shot was not a blank as you had supposed, but was in fact a live bullet which killed Mr. Tindle stone dead, spattering his blood on the banisters in the process. When you realised what you'd done, you panicked and simply buried him in the garden. It was silly of you not to wash the blood properly off the banisters and burn his clothes though.

ANDREW. I swear Tindle left here alive.

DOPPLER. I don't believe it.

ANDREW. I didn't murder him.

DOPPLER. I accept that. As I said, I think it happened by accident. We'll be quite content with a charge of manslaughter.

ANDREW. (shouting) I did not kill him! He left here alive.

DOPPLER. If you will pardon a flippancy, sir, you had better tell that to the judge.

ANDREW. Look. There's one way of settling this. If you think Tindle is in the garden, go and dig him up.

DOPPLER. We don't need to find him, sir. Recent decisions have relieved the prosecution of producing the corpus delicti. If Mr. Tindle is not under the newly turned earth in your garden, it will merely go to indicate that in your panic you first thought of putting him there, then changed your mind and buried him somewhere else.
ANDREW. Where?

DOPPLER. Does it matter? Spook Spinney! Flasher's Heath! It's all the same to us. He'll turn up sooner or later - discovered by some adulterous salesman, or rutting boy scout. And if he doesn't it scarcely matters, there's so much circumstantial evidence against you. Come along, it's time to go.

ANDREW. (a cry) No!

DOPPLER. I'm afraid I must insist, sir! There's a police car outside.

ANDREW. (louder) You may have a fleet of police cars out there. I'm not going.

DOPPLER. Now let's have no trouble, sir. Please don't make it difficult.

ANDREW. (wildly) I must see a lawyer. It's my right.

(ANDREW backs away. DOPPLER makes to seize him, there is a scuffle)

DOPPLER. You can make a call from the station, sir. We wouldn't want to do anything unconstitutional. Come on, sir. Don't despair. At the most you'll only get seven years!

ANDREW. (horrified) Seven years!

DOPPLER. Seven years to regret playing silly games that go wrong.

ANDREW. (bitterly) It didn't go wrong. It went absolutely right. You've trapped me somehow.

DOPPLER. Yes, sir. You see, we real life detectives aren't as stupid as we are sometimes portrayed by writers like yourself. We may not have our pipes, or orchid houses, our shovel hats or deer-stalkers, but we tend to be reasonably effective for all that.

ANDREW. Who the hell are you?

DOPPLER. Detective Inspector Doppler, sir, spelt as in C. Doppler 1803-1853 whose principle it was that when the source of any wave movement is approached, the frequency appears greater than it would to an observer moving away. It is also not unconnected with Doppler meaning double in German - hence Doppleganger or double image. And of course, for those whose minds run to these things, it is virtually an anagram of the word Plodder. Inspector Plodder becomes Inspector Doppler, if you see what I mean, sir!

ANDREW. (a shriek) Milo!

MILO. (normal voice) The same.

(MILO peels off his disguise which apart from elaborate face and hair make-up - wig, false nose, glasses, cheek padding and moustache, also includes a great deal of body padding, and elevator shoes, which have had the effect of making him taller than ANDREW, where in reality he is a fraction shorter)

ANDREW. You shit!

MILO. Just so.

ANDREW. You platinum plated, copper bottomed, died in the wool, all time knock down dragout, champion bastard Milo!

MILO. Thanks.

ANDREW. You weasel! You cozening coypu!

MILO. Obliged.

ANDREW. You mendacious bollock of Satan. Milo! You triple dealing turd!

MILO. In your debt.

ANDREW. Mind you, I'm not saying it wasn't well done. It was - brilliant.

MILO. Thank you.

ANDREW. Have a drink, my dear fellow?

MILO. Let me wash first. I'm covered in make-up and spirit gum.

(ANDREW shakily pours himself a whisky)

ANDREW. Just down the corridor. Cheers!

MILO. Good health. (MILO exits to bathroom U.L. as ANDREW gulps it down)

ANDREW. Yes, I must say, Milo, I congratulate you. It was first class. You really had me going there for a moment.

MILO. (offstage, quizzically) For a moment?

ANDREW. For a long moment I concede. Of course, I had my suspicions towards the end. Flasher's Heath indeed! That was going a bit far.

MILO. (offstage) I was giving you one of your English sporting chances.

ANDREW. What did you think of my performance? The anguish of an innocent man trapped by circumstantial evidence.

MILO. (offstage) Undignified - if it was a performance.

(MILO returns on stage, picks up his clothes)

ANDREW. Of course it was, and it had to be undignified to be convincing. As I say, I had my suspicions.

MILO. Indeed? How cleverly you kept them to yourself. (MILO goes upstairs to the wardrobe where he dresses in his own clothes)

ANDREW. And how well you executed it. I loved your Inspector Doppler. His relentless courtesy, his chilly rusticity, his yeoman beadiness.

MILO. (DOPPLER voice) I'm glad you view the trifling masquerade in that light, sir.

ANDREW. He was quite a masterpiece: Inspector Ringrose crossed with a hint of declasse Roger Sheringham I'd have said.

MILO. Really?

ANDREW. Oh yes. Surely you remember the Poisoned Chocolates Case 1929. It was a really astounding tour de force with no less than six separate solutions.

MILO. I've never heard of it.

ANDREW. You should read it. It's a veritable textbook of the literature. Not that you need any tips on plotting. I suppose you slipped in here when I was over in Salisbury?

MILO. Yes, I waited to see you leave.

ANDREW. And dumped the clothes in the wardrobe, and sprinkled a little sacrificial blood on the banisters.

MILO. Exactly. But it wasn't my blood you will be relieved to hear. It was obtained from a pig's liver.

ANDREW. Ugh! Perhaps you will do me the favour of wiping it off in a minute. I don't wish to fertilise the woodworm.

MILO. Question. Where would you find homosexual wood-worms?

ANDREW. What?

MILO. In a tallboy.

(ANDREW grimaces. MILO comes downstairs)

(sharply) I'd like that drink now.

ANDREW. Yes, of course. (ANDREW goes to drinks table and pours a brandy for MILO) You deserve it.

MILO. (sits on chair under staircase) You know I haven't congratulated you on your game yet. You brought it off with great elan.

ANDREW. Did you think so? Oh good! Good! I must say I was rather delighted with it myself. Tell me...did you really think that your last moment on earth had come?

75

MILO. Yes.

ANDREW. You're not angry, are you?

MILO. Anger is a meaningless word in this context.

ANDREW. I've already tried to explain it to you. I wanted to get to know you - to see if you were, as I suspected, my sort of person.

MILO. A games-playing sort of person?

ANDREW. Exactly.

MILO. And am I?

ANDREW. Most certainly. There's no doubt about it.

MILO. And what exactly is a games-playing person?

ANDREW. He's the complete man - a man of reason and imagination; of potent passions and bright fancies. He's joyous and unrepenting. His weapons are the openness of a child and the cunning of a pike and with them he faces out the black terrors of life. For me personally he is a man who dares to live his life without the crutch of domestic tension. You see, at bottom, I'm rather a solitary man. An arrangement of clouds, the secret mystery of landscape, a game of intrigue and revelation, mean more to me than people - even the ones I'm supposed to be in love with. I've never met a woman to whom the claims of intellect were as absolute as they are to me. For a long time I was reticent about all this, knowing that most people would mistake my adroit heart for one of polished stone. But it doesn't worry me any longer. I'm out in the open. I've turned my whole life into one great work of happy invention.

MILO. And you think I'm like this?

ANDREW. Yes, I do.

MILO. You're wrong.

ANDREW. I'm not. Look at the way you chose to get back at me - by playing Inspector Doppler.

MILO. That was just the need for revenge. Every Italian knows about that.

ANDREW. Rubbish. You could have revenged yourself in one of many crude Mafiosi ways - cutting off the gardener's hands, for example, or staking the cleaning woman out on the gravel, or even I suppose, as a last resort, scratched loutish words on the bonnet of my Lagonda. But no, you had to resort to a game.

MILO. I like to pay back in kind.

ANDREW. And is honour satisfied? Is it one set all?

MILO. (hard) By no means. Your game was superior to mine. I merely teased you for a few minutes with the thought of prison. (low) You virtually terrified me to death.

ANDREW. My dear fellow...

MILO. (slowly, thinking it out) And that changes you profoundly. Once you've given yourself to death, actually faced the fact that the coat sleeve button, the banister, the nail on your fourth finger, are the last things you're going to see ever - and then heard the sound of your own death - things cannot be the same again. I feel I've been tempered by madness. I stand outside and see myself for the first time without responsibility.

ANDREW. (nervous) That's shock, my dear chap. It'll pass. Here, have another drink. (ANDREW reaches for the glass. MILO jerks away. He is in great distress) How cold you are. Milo, my dear fellow, I didn't realise how absolutely cold...

MILO. So that my only duty is to even our score. That's imperative. As you would put it 'I'm three games up in the second set, having lost the first six love' That's right, isn't it? That's about how you see it? I should hate to cheat.

ANDREW. You're being too modest, Milo. In my scoring it's one set all.

MILO. Oh no, I can't accept that. You see to the ends of playing the game and drawing honourably level, I <u>have</u> killed someone.

ANDREW. Killed someone?

MILO. Murdered someone. Committed murder.

ANDREW. You're not serious.

MILO. Yes.

ANDREW. What is this. Some new murder game?

MILO. Yes. But it has a difference. Both the game and the murder are real. There's absolutely no point in another pretence murder game, is there?

ANDREW. (soothing) No, none. But I don't like to take advantage of you in this emotional state.

MILO. (shouting) It can't wait.

ANDREW. (soothing) Alright. Alright. Let's play your game. Who did you kill?

MILO. Your girlfriend, Tēa...

ANDREW. You killed Tēa?

MILO. (a little giggle) She whose cobalt eyes were the secret forest pools of Finlandia. I closed them.

ANDREW. You...

MILO. I strangled her - right here on this rug I strangled her and... I had her first.

ANDREW. You raped and str...

MILO. No. Not rape. She wanted it.

ANDREW. You're lying. You can't take me in with a crude game like this. (with braggadaccio) Honestly, Milo. You're in the big league now. I gave you credit for better sport than this.

MILO. You'll have all the sport you can stomach in a moment, Andrew. That I promise you.

ANDREW. Really, Milo, I think it would be better if...

MILO. When I was here yesterday, planning the blood and clothes for my Inspector Doppler scene, Tēa called. I strangled her. She was under that freshly dug mound of earth in the garden that so took Doppler's fancy.

ANDREW. Was? You mean she's not there now?

MILO. No. I moved her.

ANDREW. (derisory) You moved her? Where to? Flasher's Heath I suppose.

MILO. Something like that. It was too easy leaving her here... Too easy for the game you are going to play against the clock before the police arrive.

ANDREW. The police?

MILO. Yes. You see, about an hour ago I 'phoned them up and asked them to meet me here at ten o'clock tonight. They should be here in about ten minutes.

ANDREW. (sarcastic) Yes, yes. I'm sure they will be. Led, no doubt, by intrepid downy Inspector Doppler.

MILO. Oh no. It'll be a real policeman, have no fear of that. Detective Sergeant Tarrant his name is. I told him a lot about you, Andrew, I said that I knew you to be a man obsessed with games-playing and murder considered as a fine art. Your life's great ambition, I said, of which you'd often spoken, was to commit an actual real life murder, hide the body somewhere where it couldn't be traced to you and then leave clues linking you with the crime, strewn about your house in the certain knowledge that the pedestrian and simple-minded police wouldn't recognise them for what they were.

ANDREW. Obsessed with games-playing and murder considered as a fine art! That's rather ingenious of you, Milo. But it won't work. Please sir, Andrew Wyke can't rest until he's committed a real murder which is going to make fools out of all you coppers. Honestly! Tell that to the average desk Sergeant and you'll find yourself strapped straight into the giggle jacket.

MILO. Not so in fact, I told them that if they didn't believe me, one look at your bookcase and the furnishings of your house would confirm what I said about your obsessions.

ANDREW. (slow) Go on.

MILO. I also told them that two days ago your girlfriend had come to my house in great distress saying you suspected she was having affairs with other men and had threatened to kill her.

ANDREW. The police believed all that?

MILO. After some demur, yes.

ANDREW. The fuzz are watching too much T.V.

MILO. You mustn't resent imagination in public office, Andrew. Of course, I went on I had no proof that any harm had actually been done to her, but I thought I had better report the matter, particularly as I had just received an excited phone call from you, Andrew, saying you were all set to achieve your life's great ambition.

ANDREW. My dear boy, I quite appreciate you have been captivated by the spirit of games-playing and the need as you see it, to get even, but frankly you are trying too hard to be a big boy, too soon.

(ANDREW goes to the telephone and dials)

Hello, Joyce, this is Andrew. May I speak to Tēa... she what?... when was this? Where...? Oh my God!

(ANDREW replaces the receiver and takes a drink straight from the bottle. MILO is very excited)

MILO. I told you. I killed her yesterday. Now sweat for your life. You have a little over ten minutes before the law arrives. It's your giant brain against their plodding ones. Concealed in this room are two incriminating clues. And as a final expression of your contempt for the police you hid the murder weapon itself. Do you follow me so far?

ANDREW. (admiringly) You bastard!

MILO. No judgements please. Three objects. Those you don't find, be sure the police will. I should add that they're all in plain view though I have somewhat camouflaged them to make the whole thing more fun. The first object is a crystal bracelet.

ANDREW. Not...

MILO. Yes, I tore it off her wrist...off you go. It's inscribed "From Andrew to Tēa, a propitiary offering to a Karelian Goddess".

ANDREW. Alright! Alright! I know how it's inscribed.

(ANDREW takes off his jacket and starts his search)

MILO. Would you like some help?

ANDREW. Yes, damn you!

MILO. Tch! Tch! ... For any man with half an eye
What stands before him may espy;

> But optics sharp it needs I ween,
> To see what is not to be seen.

ANDREW. (furious) You said everything was in plain view.

MILO. Well, it's paradoxical old me, isn't it?

ANDREW. I'll get my own back for this... don't worry. That I promise you. I'll roast you for this... I'll make you so sorry you ever...

MILO. Eight minutes.

ANDREW. (slowly to himself) I must think... I must think... It's in plain view, yet not to be seen. H'm... there's a visual trick involved.

(ANDREW searches the stage)

MILO. A propitiary offering, eh! What was it you had to propitiate for I ask myself?

ANDREW. None of your bloody business.

MILO. Just for being yourself I suppose. Just for being cold, torturing, Andrew Wyke. Poor Tëa, I wonder if all her jewellery was inscribed with apologies for your bully boy behaviour.

ANDREW. That's a cheap jibe.

MILO. Mind you, at least you gave her some. Marguerite just had the use of them.

ANDREW. I see what you're doing. You're trying to distract me... But you won't succeed... I"ll solve your puzzle ... Let me think... Optics sharp it needs to see what is not to be seen... with the naked eye? It's microscopic! You only see a fraction of it. That's it!

(ANDREW picks up the microscope and uses it)

MILO. You won't need the Sherlock Holmes kit, Andrew. The bracelet is full sized and in full view. Though the detective angle is not a bad one. I wonder how your man, Merrydick, would have gone about the search.

ANDREW. (furious) Merrydew! St. Lord John Merrydew!

MILO. Perhaps he'd have clambered up on to that desk to look at the plinth, hauling his great tun of port belly after him.

(ANDREW climbs up on his desk to inspect the plinth)

Or perhaps he'd have gone straight to the chimney and shoved his fat Father Christmas face right up it.

(ANDREW runs to the chimney and climbs inside it)

My God! cried the noble Lord, puking on his pipe and indulging his famed taste for bad puns. This is hardly a sootable place for a gentleman!

(ANDREW emerges from the chimney)

ANDREW. I won't listen to you. I must think... What are the properties of crystal? It's hard... It's brilliant ... It's transparent.

MILO. You're getting warm, Andrew.

ANDREW. You look through it and you don't see it. Now the only place to conceal a transparent thing, so as to make it invisible yet keep it in plain view, is in another transparent thing like...

(ANDREW inspects various glass objects including Milo's drink which he is holding conspicuously. Finally he crosses to the ornamental tank, down stage right and lifts out the bracelet)

Suddenly it's all as clear as crystal. I don't need to destroy this, do I? She could have this here any time.

MILO. True, it was only planted so that the police could read the inscription. At least they'd know that your relationship with Tēa hadn't always been a happy one.

ANDREW. Very subtle. What next?

MILO. The next object is much more damning. The clue is a riddle, which goes as follows:

> Two brothers we are,
> Great burdens we bear,
> On which we are bitterly pressed.
> The truth is to say,
> We are full all the day,
> And empty when we go to rest.

ANDREW. Oh, I know that... don't tell me... full all the day, empty when we go to rest... it's a... it's a pair of shoes!

MILO. Very good. In this case, one right, high-heeled shoe. Size 6. The other, I need hardly add, is on Tēa's body.

ANDREW. Oh, my God. Poor Tēa.

(ANDREW searches the room)

MILO. Poor Tēa, eh? Well, that's a bit better. It's the first sign of sorrow you've shown since you heard of her death.

ANDREW. It's not true! You think I don't care about Tēa, don't you? But I must save myself.

MILO. You're loving it. You're in a high state of brilliance and excitement. The thought that you are playing a game for your life is practically giving you an orgasm. It's pitiable.

ANDREW. Hold your filthy tongue. What you see before you is someone using a mighty control to keep terror in check, while he tries to solve a particularly sadistic and morbid puzzle. It's a triumph of the mind over atavism!

(ANDREW searches under the stairs and in the book-shelves, and pipe racks then the sailor's foot and finally finds the shoe in a brightly decorated cornucopia attached to the stage left column)

Ah! What have we here?

MILO. Very good! Sorry it's so messy. It's only earth from Tēa's first grave in your garden.

(ANDREW burns the shoe in the stove)

ANDREW. Now there's one thing left, isn't there. The murder weapon, that's what you said. Now you strangled her here. What with? Let's see... a rope ... a belt... a scarf...

MILO. It bit into her neck very deeply, Andrew. I had to prise it loose.

ANDREW. You sadistic bloody wop!

MILO. I hope I didn't hear that correctly... It would be foolish to antagonise me at this stage. Because as you're certain to need a lot more help, I would hate to have to give you an oblique, Florentine sort of clue, sewn with treachery and double dealing.

ANDREW. (controlling himself) Alright! Alright!

MILO. As Don Quixote in common with a great number of chaps remarked, "No es Oro todo que reluce".

ANDREW. But the other chaps of course, didn't say it in Spanish, did they?

MILO. Well at least you know it was Spanish, even if you can't speak it. I suppose that's what is meant by a general education in England.

ANDREW. God, you're pretty damned insufferable, Milo.

MILO. I've learnt it. Let's try you on a little Latin. Every gentleman knows Latin. I'm sure you're acquainted with the Winchester College Hall Book of 1401 ?

ANDREW. (sarcastic) Naturally. As a matter of fact I've got the paperback by my bedside.

MILO. (bland) Then you will remember an entry by Alanus De Insulis - "Non teneas nurum totum quod splendet ut aurum".

ANDREW. (sarcastic) I'm afraid I can't have got that far yet.

MILO. Pity... I suppose I could put it another way. "Que tout n'est pas or qu'on voit luire". The French, of course, is thirteenth century.

ANDREW. Say it again, slowly.

MILO. All-that-glitters...

ANDREW. All that glitters isn't gold... Why didn't you say that in the first place...

(MILO whistles a scale)

Golden notes? Golden whistle?... Golden cord?... Golden cord! You strangled her with a golden cord and put it round the bell pull.

(ANDREW runs to the bell pull, examines it, but finds nothing)

No you didn't.

(MILO whistles "Anything Goes")

Anything goes. In olden d... In olden days a... glimpse of stocking. It's in the spin dryer.

86

(ANDREW goes off down corridor to kitchen)

MILO. Cold, cold. It's in this room remember.

ANDREW. Where do you put stockings? On legs, golden legs...

(ANDREW examines the golden legs of the fender, then a chair)

MILO. (sings) "In olden days a glimpse of stocking was looked on as something shocking..." I thought I heard something.

(MILO exits to hallway. MILO comes back on stage)

Yes, Andrew, it's the police. They're coming up the drive.

ANDREW. (desperate) Keep them out! Give me one more minute!

MILO. A glimpse of stocking, remember.

(MILO exits to hallway)

(off stage) Good evening. Detective Sergeant Tarrant.

DET. SGT. TARRANT. Yes, sir. This is Constable Higgs.

MILO. Good evening, Constable.

CON. HIGGS. Good evening, sir.

(The grandfather clock strikes 10.00)

ANDREW. Olden days... A glimpse... Now you see it now you don't! Of course, the clock.

(He rushes to clock and finds stocking)

MILO. Nice of you to be so prompt. I apologise for keeping you waiting out there for a moment. The front door's a bit stiff.

TARRANT. That's alright, sir. We're used to waiting.

MILO. Won't you hang your coats up? It's a bit warm inside.

TARRANT. Thank you, sir. I expect we'll be here a little time.

(ANDREW puts stocking into fire)

MILO. Here, Constable. Let me take your helmet.

HIGGS. Thank you, sir. If it's all the same to you, I think I'll keep it with me, but I'll take my coat off. (Door slams off-stage. ANDREW runs to his desk and sits unconcernedly reading)

MILO. Come in, gentlemen. May I introduce Mr. Andrew Wyke. Andrew, may I introduce Detective Sergeant Tarrant and Constable Higgs.

ANDREW. Come in, gentlemen, come in.

(A pause. No one enters)

MILO. Or perhaps I should say Inspector Plodder and Constable Freshface. Thank you, Sergeant. We won't be needing you after all.

TARRANT'S VOICE. That's alright, sir. Better to be safe than sorry, that's what I say. Good night, sir.

MILO. (own voice) Good night, Sergeant. Good night, Constable. Good night, sir.

(ANDREW sinks on the settee, shattered)

Aren't you going to ask about Tēa? She did call here yesterday looking for you when I was here setting the Doppler scene. I told her about the trick you had played on me with the gun. She wasn't a bit surprised.

She knows only too well the kind of games you play -
the kind of humiliation you enjoy inflicting on people.
I said I wanted to play a game to get even with you and
I asked her to help me. I asked her to lend me a
stocking, a shoe and a bracelet. She collaborated with
enthusiasm. So did her flat-mate, Joyce. Would you
like to telephone her, she'll talk to you now? Of
course you don't really have much to say to her, do
you? She's not really your mistress She told me you
and she hadn't slept together for over a year. She told
me you were practically impotent - not at all, in fact,
the selector's choice for the next Olympics.

(ANDREW hides his head as MILO starts up the stairs)

ANDREW. Where are you going?

MILO. To collect Marguerite's fur coat.

ANDREW. She's not coming back?

MILO. No. Among other things she said she was fed up
with living in Hamleys.

ANDREW. Hamleys?

MILO. It's a toy shop in Regent Street.

ANDREW. Milo.

MILO. Yes?

ANDREW. Don't go. Don't waste it all on Marguerite.
She doesn't appreciate you like I do. You and I are
evenly matched. We know what it is to play a game
and that's so rare. Two people coming together who
have the courage to spend the little time of light between
the eternal darkness - joking.

MILO. Do you mean live here?

ANDREW. Yes.

MILO. (scornfully) Is it legal in private between two consenting games-players?

ANDREW. Please... I just want someone to play with.

MILO. No.

ANDREW. Please.

MILO. No. Most people want someone to live with. But you have no life to give anyone - only tricks and the shadows of long ago. Take a look at yourself, Andrew, and ask yourself a few simple questions about your attachment to the English detective story. Perhaps you might come to realise that the only place you can inhabit is a dead world - a country house world where peers and colonels die in their studies; where butlers steal the port, and pert parlourmaids cringe, weeping malopropisms behind green baize doors. It's a world of coldness and class hatred, and two dimensional characters who are not expected to communicate; it's a world where only the amateurs win, and where foreigners are automatically figures of fun. To be puzzled is all. Forgive me for taking Marguerite to a life where people try to understand. To put it shortly, the detective story is the normal recreation of snobbish, out-dated, life hating, ignoble minds. I'll get that fur coat now. I presume it is Marguerite's, unless, that is, you've taken to transvestisism as a substitute for non-performance.

(MILO disappears into the bedroom. ANDREW sits on below, crushed and humiliated. After a minute, he rises and starts wearily across the stage. Suddenly he stops as a thought enters his mind)

ANDREW. (to himself) The coat!... The fur coat... of course... I've got him!

(He brightens visibly - a man who realises suddenly that he can rescue a victory out of the jaws of defeat - and crosses firmly to his desk and takes out his gun)

You see, Inspector, I was working in the morning room
when I heard a noise. I seized my gun and came in
here. I saw the figure of a man, apparently carrying
my wife's fur coat. I shouted for him to put his hands
up, but instead he ran towards the front door, trying
to escape. Though I aimed low, I'm afraid I shot him
dead.

(INSPECTOR's voice) Mustn't blame yourself, sir,
could have happened to anybody!

(MILO returns carrying fur coat. He comes down the
stairs, but does not see the gun hidden behind ANDREW's
back)

I'm not going to let you go, you know.

MILO. No? What are you going to do, Andrew. Shoot me
down? Play that old burglar game again?

ANDREW. Yes, that's precisely what I could do.

MILO. It wouldn't work, you know, even if you had the guts
to go through with it.

ANDREW. Why not?

(MILO fetches a suitcase from the hall and packs the
fur coat)

MILO. Because of what happened when I left here on Friday
night. I lurched home in the moonlight, numb and dazed,
and soiled. I sat up all night in a chair - damaged -
contaminated by you and this house. I remembered
something my father said to me; "In this country, Milo"
he said, "there's justice, but sometimes for a foreigner
it is difficult". In the morning I went to the police
station and told them what had happened. One of them
- Sergeant Tarrant - yes he's real - took me into a
room and we had quite a long chat. But I don't think he
really believed me, even though I showed him the powder
burn on my head. He seemed more interested in my
relationship with Marguerite, which by the way they all

appeared to know about. I felt this terrible anger
coming over me. I thought "they're not going to believe
me because I'm a stranger from London who's screwing
the wife of the local nob and has got what he deserved".
So I thought of my father, and what I might have done
in Italy, and I took my own revenge. But remember,
Andrew, the police might still come.

ANDREW. (slowly) Then why haven't they, then?

MILO. I don't know, perhaps they won't. But even if they
don't, you can't play your burglar game now, they'd
never swallow it. So you see you've lost.

ANDREW. I don't believe one word you're saying.

MILO. (deliberately) It's the truth.

ANDREW. You're lying.

MILO. Why don't you 'phone Sergeant Tarrant if you don't
believe me.

ANDREW. And say what? Please Sergeant has Milo Tindle
been in saying that I framed him as a burglar and then
shot him. I'm not that half-witted.

MILO. Suit yourself.

ANDREW. I shall shoot you, Milo. You come here and ask
my permission to steal away my wife, you pry into my
manhood, you lecture me on dead worlds and ignoble
minds, and you mock Merridew. Well, they're all real
bullets this time.

MILO. I'm going home now.

(MILO starts to leave, ANDREW fires at the last
moment. MILO staggers downstage right and drops
in pain, fatally. ANDREW kneels and holds his head up)

ANDREW. You're a bad liar, Milo, and in the final analysis,
an uninventive games-player. Can you hear me? Then

listen to this, NEVER play the same game three times running!

(There is the sound of a car approaching and pulling to a halt. A flashy blue police car light shines through the window. The door bell rings. Loud knocking on door. Painfully MILO lifts his head from the floor, he laughs)

MILO. Game, set and match!

(His laugh becomes a cough. Blood trickles from his mouth. He grimaces in surprise at the pain and dies. The knocking on the door is repeated more loudly. ANDREW staggers to his desk and accidentally presses the button on it. This sets off the sailor who laughs ironically. The knocking becomes more insistent. ANDREW leans weakly against pillar as the curtain falls)

MARAT/SADE

The Persecution and Assassination of Marat as performed by the inmates of the Asylum of Charenton under the direction of the Marquis de Sade

by Peter Weiss

This powerful and savage play, the climactic expression of Artaud's 'Theatre of Cruelty', combines Sadeian philosophy, and the discipline of verse with a range of theatrical shock techniques. No play by a German since Brecht has enjoyed the success of *Marat/Sade*, and its author, Peter Weiss, was one of the most remarkable of the post-war generation of German writers. This English version by Geoffrey Skelton and Adrian Mitchell was the text used in Peter Brook's brilliant production for the Royal Shakespeare Company.

Peter Weiss was born in Berlin in 1916 and settled in Sweden before the war. Apart from his writing, he was a well-known painter, theatrical and operatic producer and he directed many films in Sweden. He died in 1982.

ISBN: 9780714503615
Paperback
£8.95

THE INVESTIGATION
by Peter Weiss

The Investigation is a dramatic reconstruction of the Frankfurt War Crimes trials, based on the actual evidence given. This testimony, concerning Auschwitz and the atrocities which were enacted there, has been edited and extracted by Peter Weiss into a dramatic document that relies solely and completely on the facts for its effectiveness.

There is no artistic license, no manipulation of facts and figures, no rearrangement of events for theatrical effect. Nameless witnesses stand and recall their appalling memories of Auschwitz, allowing us to bear witness to their painful and painstaking search for truth and ultimately justice. What emerges is a chastening and purging documentary of deeply moving power.

Peter Weiss was born in Berlin in 1916 and settled in Sweden before the war. Apart from his writing, he was a well-known painter, theatrical and operatic producer and he directed many films in Sweden. He died in 1982.

ISBN: 9780714503011
Paperback
£8.95/$14.95